Carnival in Costa Rica 1947

Words and Music 1948

Let's Be Happy 1957

Three Little Girls in Blue 1946

Call Me Madam 1953

Three Little Words 1950

White Christmas
1954

Three Little Words
1950

White Christmas
1954

White Christmas
1954

The Belle of New York
1952

Three Little Words
1950

All, *White Christmas* 1954 ...with Rosemary Clooney

The Kid from Brooklyn 1946

Three Little Girls in Blue 1946

Happy Go Lovely 1951

Call Me Madam
1953

The Belle of New York
1952

Three Little Words
1950